STRANGE ANIMALS, NEW TO SCIENCE

STRANGE ANIMALS, NEW TO SCIENCE

Laurence Pringle

MARSHALL CAVENDISH   NEW YORK

Library of Congress Cataloging-in-Publication Data
Pringle, Laurence P.
Strange animals, new to science/Laurence Pringle.
p.   cm.
ISBN 0-7614-5083-1
1. Rare animals—Juvenile literature. [1. Rare animals. 2, Animals.] I. Title.
QL83.P75 2001   591.68—dc21   2001028185

The text of this book is set in 13 point Berkeley Old Style Medium.
Printed in Malaysia
First edition
3 5 6 4 2

Cover photos: top, Lina's Sunbird, Allan P. Sutherland, © Cincinnati Museum Center;
bottom, Leaf deer, Alan Rabinowitz

The photographs in this book are used by permission and through the courtesy of: Doug Wechsler, VIREO, 13;
World Wildlife Fund, 17; J.M. Lammertink, 18; Peter Zahler, 22; Allan P. Sutherland, © Cincinnati Museum
Center, 25; Robert S. Kennedy, © Cincinnati Museum Center, 26; Farah Ishtiaq, 29; John Lundberg, 32, 33;
Summer Arrigo-Nelson, 35; Alan Rabinowitz, 38, 51; Robert Timmins, 40; Eduardo Brettas, 43; Tim Flannery,
48; Marc van Roosmalen, Conservation International, 54

CONTENTS

STRANGE ANIMALS, NEW TO SCIENCE

Monkeys in South America, a barking deer in Vietnam, one of the world's smallest frogs in Cuba—these are all animals recently discovered on Earth. In the past two decades many unfamiliar animals and plants have been found by scientists.

Even as you read these words, somewhere on Earth biologists are exploring tropical forests, ocean depths, and other wild habitats. Their discoveries will add to a fast-growing list of newly named species and of others that were believed to have become extinct but have been found alive.

Throughout history, humans have been fascinated to learn about the existence of species new to them. In the early1800s, for example, President Thomas Jefferson and many other people living in the eastern United States eagerly awaited the report of the Lewis and Clark expedition, which ascended the Missouri River, crossed the Rocky Mountains, reached the Pacific Ocean, and returned in 1806. The journals of Lewis and Clark described many unfamiliar plants and animals, including the western rattlesnake, pronghorn, mountain goat, mule deer, and prairie dog. Two new species of birds were named after the expedition's leaders: Lewis's woodpecker and Clark's nutcracker.

As time passed, however, and more of the world was explored and settled, it seemed that most of Earth's animals had been discovered. In 1970 the tally of vertebrates (animals with backbones) included about 4,000 mammals, 19,000 fishes, 9,000 birds, and more than 10,000 reptiles and amphibians. Then and now, biologists believed that the animals remaining to be identified would be mostly insects, spiders, and other creatures without backbones (invertebrates).

Nevertheless, each year a few new vertebrate species were discovered. In 1973, for example, the world's smallest mammal—the bumblebee bat—was found living in a small area of Thailand. One of these tiny bats weighs about as much as a United States penny. In 1976 a large shark with a huge mouth was captured for the first time off Hawaii. Since then only a few specimens of this unusual deepwater species, called the megamouth shark, have been caught.

In the late 1980s biologists began searching for new species with increased urgency. They felt that time was running out. All over Earth, wildlife habitats were being destroyed at an alarming rate. As tropical forests and other habitats disappeared, so did untold numbers of plants and animals, including species that became extinct even before they had been identified. (Extinctions have always occurred, but the mass extinction now underway is caused by humanmade changes in the environment.)

Many people are alarmed at the rapid loss of Earth's variety of life— its biodiversity. Biologists are searching for new species before they disappear. In the process they are sometimes delighted to find animals or plants that were thought to be extinct. They also seek to identify areas that are especially rich in biodiversity so that these habitats— and the plants and animals living in them—might be saved.

The hunt for new species has produced amazing results. The discovery of new kinds of bats, rodents, monkeys, and other mammals has raised the total to more than 4,600 mammalian species, and some biologists estimate that as many as 3,000 other mammals remain to be found. The estimates of unknown birds, reptiles, fishes, and other vertebrates have also increased.

The same is true of insects and other invertebrates—and of plants. In 1994 a hiker in Australia's Wollemi National Park found a small grove of unusual trees in a rain forest gorge. The trees were known only from fossil leaf imprints in rocks, and were believed to have become extinct 50 million years ago. An Australian botanist said that the discovery was equal to "finding a small dinosaur still alive on Earth."

The trees have been named Wollemi pines, after the national park where they grow. Wollemi is an Aboriginal word that means "look around you." The following pages tell how biologists continue to "look around" and about some of the fascinating animals they have found.

THE JOCOTOCO ANTPITTA
OF ECUADOR

Experienced bird watchers often identify birds by their sounds. Each species has distinctive calls, as well as a unique song or other sounds it makes during its mating season. This is a great help when people try to identify birds in dense thickets or other habitats where visibility is poor.

In 1997 two ornithologists (biologists who study birds) were listening to bird calls as they hiked down a trail on the forested eastern slope of the Andes Mountains in southern Ecuador. "You hear about ten times as many birds as you see," recalls Robert Ridgely, an ornithologist at the Academy of Natural Sciences in Philadelphia. He was accompanied by John Moore, an expert in recording bird songs.

They heard an odd bird call—distant but loud, something like the hoot of an owl. Then nothing more. The two ornithologists continued walking, hoping to hear the mysterious sound again. They suspected that a familiar Ecuadorian bird was giving a call that hadn't been noticed before. They were, after all, on a well-traveled path near the border of a national park that was often visited by bird watchers—not a likely place to encounter a new species.

A few minutes later, walking on, they heard the strange call again. This time Robert Ridgely flicked on his microphone and recorded the last few seconds of the sound.

Suddenly, a bird with a body about the size of a grapefruit appeared out of the undergrowth. The bird hopped on long legs. The upper parts of its round body were covered with black and brown feathers. It had a pure white patch of feathers under its beak and under each eye. Ridgely says, "It didn't look like anything I'd ever encountered. It was stunningly different. I whispered to John: 'My God! It's a new species!'"

The bird quickly disappeared among the jungle of plants on the forest floor, leaving the two men with the challenge of proving they had just met a species unknown to ornithology. A brief sighting would not do. To officially confirm that an animal species exists, one or more individuals must be caught, killed, and preserved so they can be studied and compared with other bird specimens in science museums. Also, an exact, detailed description, a scientific name, and information about the animal's life, habitat, and place of discovery must be published in a scientific journal.

The men were scheduled to leave the area the next day, but in the morning hurried back to the place where they had seen the bird. The weather was cold and rainy, as it often is high on the eastern mountain slopes of the Andes.

At an altitude of 11,000 feet above sea level, clouds are often at ground level, so the lush growth is called cloud forest.

Over and over again, Ridgely and Moore played the recording of the bird's voice made the previous day. After about an hour, one of the strange birds appeared. Ridgely was able to take some photographs before it vanished into the vegetation.

Those photographs enabled Ridgely to get permission from the Ecuadorian government to catch some of the birds. While he was back in the United States, an Ecuadorian ornithologist (who had been trained by Ridgely) managed to catch one. Early in 1998 Ridgely

returned with a team of researchers and photographer Doug Wechsler. They were able to capture more of the birds, and Wechsler took the first clear, close-up photographs of one.

The newly identified species is called the jocotoco antpitta. Jocotoco is a name given to the bird when local Ecuadorians hear its call. It is an unusually large member of the antbird family. This group of birds is named for the feeding behavior of some species, which eat insects and other invertebrates that are fleeing from army ants. There are no army ants where the jocotoco antpitta lives, but it does eat insects.

Robert Ridgely has been the first to identify other bird species, but calls the jocotoco antpitta "far and away the most exciting discovery of my career." The bird was first seen on private land outside the boundaries of Podocarpus National Park. (The park is named for the podocarpus, a coniferous, cone-bearing tree that grows tall in the cloud forest of Ecuador.) Logging and gold mining threaten most of the wild habitat in the region near the national park. The survival of the jocotoco antpitta and countless other cloud forest animals and plants depends on protecting their habitat.

A STONE AGE HORSE IN TIBET

In October 1995 a scientific expedition explored on horseback deep in Tibet, south of the Chinese border. The route through mountain passes was blocked by an early snow storm, so the caravan had to take a different, rarely traveled path. In an isolated valley they came upon herds of small horses about the size of ponies. The light brown horses had black legs and a black stripe on their backs. The French leader of the expedition, Michel Peissel, said, "They looked completely archaic, like the horses in prehistoric cave paintings."

The horses were named the Riwoche (ree-woe-chay) breed, after the long valley in which they were discovered. They were not completely unknown to people. Tibetan farmers in the valley caught these horses when they needed them to ride or to serve as pack animals, then set them free. However, the horses were unknown to the world outside the Riwoche region of Tibet. Their valley is cut off by mountain passes 16,000 feet (4,800 meters) high where there is no grass that would be needed for food by traveling horses. It appears that the Riwoche horses have been isolated for thousands of years, and have not interbred with other varieties of Tibetan horses, which are very different.

In Tibet the expedition also found an unusual high-altitude forest of enormous trees inhabited by rare white-lipped deer and by medium-size macaque monkeys that foraged for food under the snow. Although the deer and monkeys were known species, this wild, little-explored habitat may prove to be the home of varieties of plants and animals never before seen by scientists.

THE JAVAN RHINOCEROS
OF VIETNAM

The Javan rhinoceros once lived throughout Southeast Asia, but its numbers dropped lower and lower as hunters killed the rhinos for their horns. Ground-up rhino horn is highly valued in Chinese folk medicine, and rhino horn is also made into decorative dagger handles. Eventually only a few rhinos survived—one subspecies in Vietnam, another in Java, Indonesia. Today fewer than 70 of the Indonesian subspecies live in a Java national park.

Little was known about the Vietnam subspecies when it was reported to be extinct early in the twentieth century. Hopes for its survival were dashed by the Vietnam War of the 1960s, when large areas of wild forest habitat in Vietnam were bombed, sprayed with Agent Orange (a plant-killing poison), and strewn with land mines.

In the decades after the war, however, there were occasional reports of rhino sightings in Vietnam. A team of photographers and scientists from the World Wildlife Fund went to Vietnam in 1999 to investigate. They found rhino footprints in a wild bamboo forest in southern Vietnam, but saw none of the wary rhinos, which are active at night. The photographers set up ten cameras in areas where they believed the rhinos might live. Whenever an animal broke a beam of infrared light in front of a camera, a flash photograph was taken. Day after day passed, and they found only photographs of civets, wild pigs, sambar deer, gaur, and muntjacs. Finally, after two weeks a live Javan rhinoceros was captured on film.

Although biologists were delighted that a reportedly extinct animal was still alive, they are worried about its survival. No more than fifteen individuals of the species are known to exist. They live in the Cat Loc Nature Reserve, but the park was not well protected against people clearing trees for farming. The World Wildlife Fund and other conservation groups are working with the Vietnamese government and local communities to protect the wild habitat that rhinos need. Worldwide these groups also support efforts to stop illegal killing of rhinos, and to stem trade in products made of rhinoceros horn.

A NEW CUBAN FROG

The island nation of Cuba is home to about sixty species of frogs, most of which live nowhere else on Earth. In 1993 Cuban zoologist Alberto Estrada did not expect to find yet another species when he heard high-pitched chirps coming from beneath ferns on a remote mountain in eastern Cuba. The chirps came from tiny orange-striped black frogs. After collecting and examining several of the frogs, he conferred with a biologist with whom he often explored Cuban rain forests, Blair Hedges of Pennsylvania State University. In 1996 Estrada and Hedges officially announced the discovery of a new frog species—the smallest in the Northern Hemisphere. In fact, this Cuban frog is tied with a frog found in Brazil in 1971 for the title of smallest frog in the world.

The Cuban frog measures about two-fifths of an inch (10 mm) in length. It can easily perch on a United States dime (which is 17 mm across). Because it is so tiny, the frog probably escapes the attention of snakes and other predators that eat frogs. However, it may be hunted by centipedes and spiders.

Like any newly discovered species, the tiny frog's life is mostly a mystery. And like many species of frogs, iguanas, butterflies, and other animals that live only on the island nation of Cuba, the frog's survival depends on conservation of Cuba's remaining wild habitat. About ninety percent of Cuba's forests has been cut down or burned. If steps are not taken to halt their destruction, Blair Hedges said, "The forests are going, and the little frog is going with them."

THE WOOLLY FLYING SQUIRREL OF PAKISTAN

In North America and around the world, flying squirrels nest in trees. Sometimes they spread their legs wide, stretching out "wings" of loose skin on each side, and glide from one branch or tree to another. The two North American species usually measure no more than a foot (30 centimeters) long and weigh less than half a pound (a quarter of a kilogram).

A much larger flying squirrel—the woolly flying squirrel—was once known to exist in Pakistan. It was the largest squirrel of any kind in the world. Its tail alone measured two feet (60 cm) long. This unusual species was discovered in 1888. A few skins and skeletons were preserved in museums. Almost nothing was known about the life of this remarkable mammal. By the early 1990s the woolly flying squirrel was generally thought to be extinct; the last recorded sighting by a Westerner, a British colonel, occurred in 1924.

A few biologists wondered if it had somehow survived. One who was writing a book about the mammals of Pakistan searched "in all sorts of high valleys in the mountains," without success. In 1992 another person began to search. Peter Zahler, a conservation biologist now at the University of Massachusetts, wrote that "curiosity overcame common sense and I headed for the Himalayas." He set out baited live traps in remote mountain valleys but saw no squirrels. He returned in 1994 with enough money from the World Wildlife

Fund for two months of exploration. He was assisted by Chantal Dietemann, a college mathematics teacher.

More than a month passed without success. Then they tried a new area and Chantal Dietemann found an unusually large squirrel-like paw on top of a cliff. Could it be from a woolly flying squirrel that had been killed and eaten by a predator? The paw was a tantalizing but frustrating clue unless more evidence could be found. A few days later, two men from the area walked into camp and told Zahler they could catch one of the squirrels alive. Peter Zahler was skeptical but offered a reward. He loaned them a sack. In a few hours the men returned the sack—with a live female woolly flying squirrel inside!

After the animal had been examined, measured, and photographed, she was released alive near the cave where she had been caught. Peter Zahler and Chantal Dietemann never saw another live squirrel in 1994, though they found bones and other remains of several beneath the roost of an eagle owl. In the years that followed, Peter Zahler (now at the Department of Forestry and Wildlife, University of Massachusetts, and also a Research Associate with The Wildlife Conservation Society) returned to Pakistan several times. By the year 2000 he had captured eight woolly flying squirrels and was learning more about the species' behavior and foods. However, its habit of sleeping in cliff caves in daytime and foraging in trees at night has kept much of its life a mystery. Zahler did see some squirrels gliding—to avoid capture— in the daytime. One woolly flying squirrel glided from one side of a canyon to the opposite side, a distance of about 500 feet (150 m)— the length of about one-and-a-half football fields.

In Pakistan, Peter Zahler has spent most of his time developing a conservation plan for the area. He has trained teachers and in other

ways encouraged the local people of this rugged, remote area to save some forest habitat and the wildlife that depends on it. His goal, and that of other conservation biologists, is to convince people that protecting wildlife habitats is in their best interest—now and for generations to come.

LINA'S SUNBIRD AND THE PANAY CLOUDRUNNER OF THE PHILIPPINES

The rain forests of the Philippines are being rapidly destroyed, and with them a rich diversity of life is being lost. One scientist who is racing the chainsaws of loggers to discover unknown species is Robert Kennedy, a researcher at the Cincinnati Museum of Natural History & Science. He has led more than thirty expeditions to the Philippines, and is co-director of the Philippine Biodiversity Inventory with zoologist Pedro Gonzales.

In 1993, on the island of Mindanao, they collected what seemed to be an unknown species of the group called sunbirds. More than 120 species of colorful sunbirds occur in Africa and Southeast Asia. With their long, curved bills, sunbirds sip nectar from flowers. The new species was spectacular—green above and yellow below, with orange patches on its chest and belly, and with bright red eyes.

To confirm that the sunbird was a new species, Kennedy and Gonzales checked collections of bird skins in natural history museums. To their surprise, they discovered that the same species had been collected in 1965. However, it had been misidentified and labeled as another kind of sunbird from Mindanao. So Kennedy and Gonzales had indeed discovered a new species. They named it Lina's sunbird, after the wife of a famous Philippine ornithologist.

Lina's sunbird lives in mountain moss forest that seems safe from

logging because few trees of commercial value grow there. However, the loss of other kinds of forest is wiping out many species in the Philippines. For example, two species of tree-climbing rodents were discovered in the early 1980s, but one already is believed to be extinct. It lived only on a small island near Mindoro, where all of its forest habitat was destroyed.

Since 1895, scientists have known that at least one other species of tree-climbing rodent lives in the Philippines. It is called the bushy-tailed cloud rat and still survives in the highest mountains of northern Luzon. In 1992, Robert Kennedy and Pedro Gonzales confirmed the existence of a fourth species of tree-climbing rodent. A single specimen of this mammal had been collected in 1987 by people on the large island of Panay in the central Philippines. No others were found until 1992 and 1993, when local residents brought the biologists several live mammals they had captured in rugged mountain habitats.

The squirrel-like mammals measured about 26 inches (65 cm) long, including 15 to 16 inches (40 cm) of furry black tail. They had small eyes and ears, and brownish gray fur that was long and soft. This new species is related to the bushy-tailed cloud rat. However, because of its appealing looks—more like a squirrel than a rat—Robert Kennedy named it the Panay cloudrunner. Three live cloudrunners were brought to the United States to live at the Cincinnati Zoo. They are very shy animals, and are not on public display.

In the wild, cloudrunners sleep within holes in big trees during the day. They emerge at night and feed on leaves and also on bananas, guavas, and other fruits. They are fairly common in the farmland and mountain forests that remain on the island of Panay.

THE FOREST OWLET OF INDIA

For more than a century the forest owlet was considered a mystery bird in India. This small owl, just eight inches (20 cm) tall, was first identified in the 1870s. In the following dozen years, seven of the owls were collected. Their preserved remains were saved in science museums. After 1884, however, there were no confirmed sightings of the owl. It seemed to be another sad case of a species that went extinct before anyone had learned much about its life.

"Could it still exist?" wondered Pamela Rasmussun, an ornithologist at the National Museum of Natural History in Washington, D.C. Intrigued by the possibility that the owl was still alive, in 1997 she traveled to India with Ben King, an expert on Asian birds at the American Museum of Natural History in New York, and David Abbott, a bird watcher from Virginia.

They began their search in forested sites where the owlets had last been found, more than a century ago. Because the owlets had been collected in a variety of forests, they looked in different habitats. They looked for resting owlets by day, and sometimes stayed up all night listening for any owl calls that differed from the known calls of other owl species.

No owlets were found at the eastern sites. The ornithologists were beginning to lose hope as they traveled to the western sites near Shahada, northeast of Bombay. Most of the lowland forests there were gone. Nevertheless, one midmorning, Ben King looked through his binoculars at a bird in a treetop and said, "Look at that owlet!" It was

indeed the first one seen by ornithologists since 1884. Another individual was seen the next day. The biologists took still photographs and videotape of the birds. Pamela Rasmussen suspected that the two birds were a breeding pair.

She returned the following summer, found owlets at the same site, and managed to make tape recordings of their calls. Since then Farah Ishtiaq of the Bombay Natural History Society has located several more pairs and studied their nesting behavior. The rediscovered India owlet is no longer the mystery bird of India.

ELECTRIC FISH OF THE AMAZON

For centuries, explorers have traveled the mighty Amazon River to reach the interior of South America. Many other rivers flow into the Amazon, and with it form a vast drainage basin of some 2.5 million square miles (6.5 sq km). Biologists, too, have used this river system as a watery highway in their studies of rain forest plants and animals. And the rivers themselves are habitats for a great variety of fish.

The biologists who study fish—ichthyologists—have identified many kinds of fish that live only in South America. They have caught several kinds of fish that produce electricity within their bodies. They also found surprising numbers of fish that feed on fruit, leaves, seeds, and other plant materials that fall into the water along riverbanks. In the rainy season, when the Amazon overflows its banks, fish spread out for miles in the surrounding forest and feast on fruits and other plant foods.

Ichthyologists estimate that there may be as many as 5,000 species of freshwater fishes in the vast Amazon basin—twice the number found in all of Mexico, Canada, and the United States. They are confident that unknown fish species can be found right in the main channels of the Amazon and its largest tributaries. These waters are like little-explored frontiers because of their depth and swift currents, as well as sunken trees that rip holes in fishing nets.

Ichthyologist John Lundberg was advised to bring plenty of nets when he began a series of expeditions to study Amazon fishes in 1992. He teamed up with Brazilian fish researchers. They dropped weighted

fine mesh nets into water that raced along at speeds of six feet
(1.8 m) or more per second. As they retrieved a net from thirty to 150
feet (9–45 m) below the surface, they could not see their catch until
the net was lifted from the muddy brown water of the Amazon.

The murky depths of the Amazon are nearly lightless, like a cave.
The researchers netted many kinds of catfish and electric fish, none
of which relied on sight to find food. Some species had tiny eyes or
lacked eyes entirely.

One species of blind catfish was only two inches (5 cm) long.
Totally lacking color, its body was transparent. The smallest species
of blind catfish measured less than half an inch long (11 mm).
Catfish have taste buds all over their bodies; many are also able to
detect tiny electrical charges given off by other living things. These
senses enable blind catfish, blind or sighted, big or little, to find food
and to navigate in the Amazon's dark waters.

John Lundberg and the Brazilian ichthyologists discovered several remarkable species of electric fishes. Like all electric fish, they have organs that produce electric fields around their bodies that help the fish sense their surroundings. The biologists caught some electric fish that appeared to be individuals of one species, except some were solid-colored and others were mottled. However, the fish were found to have distinct patterns of electrical discharges, showing that they were two new species.

It is impossible for scientists to observe the behavior of electric fish living in the murky depths of the Amazon. By examining stomach contents, however, they can learn what the fish have eaten. They discovered two different species whose stomachs were filled with the tails of other electric fish! Since electric fish quickly grow new tails, the tail-eaters did not greatly harm their prey. The tail-eating electric fish were harvesting a crop that grew again.

THE GOLDEN BAMBOO LEMUR
OF MADAGASCAR

In 1978, Patricia Wright was the first biologist to study the behavior of wild owl monkeys (which are active at night) in a remote Peruvian forest. By 1985 she had observed monkeys in the forests of Asia, Africa, and South America. That year she traveled to Madagascar. Flying over this large island, east of Africa, she saw very little wild forest. Most of it had been cut or burned to clear the land for growing rice. The loss of these forests had also caused the extinction of many species, including lemurs that lived nowhere else on Earth.

Lemurs are primates, related to monkeys, apes, and humans. They live only on Madagascar and on the nearby Comores Islands. Patricia Wright and other primatologists (scientists who study primates) had come to Madagascar in 1985 to study lemurs, and to look for one species that was thought to be extinct. The greater bamboo lemur had not been seen by scientists for more than thirty years. Since it had been known to eat bamboo, she searched bamboo-covered slopes of the Ranomafana rainforest in southeastern Madagascar.

For weeks she looked in vain for the greater bamboo lemur—a dark gray mammal with white ear tufts. Then, one misty morning, she heard sounds—whirring, purring, cawing sounds—that she had never heard before. She looked up and saw a strange creature clinging to a bamboo limb. It was smaller than the lemur for which she was searching. It was rust-colored, "with chipmunk cheeks and teddy-bear

ears. And there it is, in front of me, whirling its tail around in a circle scolding me with a harsh cluck, and then it's gone."

The mysterious lemur was wary of humans and was not seen again for several days. Patricia Wright spent three months trying to locate and observe this lemur and its family. "They were very good at hiding," she recalls. "Sometimes when I lost them, it would take days of searching before I could find them again. But finally the lemur and its family became used to seeing me, and it was easier to study them."

She learned that these lemurs ate mostly the young shoots of bamboo. These shoots are rich in cyanide, a chemical that is poisonous to humans, but does not harm this lemur species. To Patricia Wright, discovering an unknown species was like finding a rich treasure in the forest, so she named it the golden bamboo lemur. About two thousand are known to exist.

Several months later Patricia Wright also found small numbers of the greater bamboo lemur. It was still alive, not extinct, but like the golden bamboo lemur and other living treasures of Madagascar, it will not survive unless its forest habitat is protected.

THE SAOLA OF VIETNAM

In 1992 a team of scientists from the World Wildlife Fund and from Vietnam began exploring one of the last untouched wild habitats in northern Vietnam—the Vu Quang Nature Reserve. Its rugged, rain-drenched forests lie along Vietnam's mountainous border with Laos. The area was picked for study because satellite photographs showed that it was remarkably untouched by logging or other use by people.

The biologists found several new species of fish and birds, and a tortoise. However, the first clue to a truly extraordinary discovery was found not in the forest but in a village. British biologist John MacKinnon saw an unusual skull hanging on the wall in a hunter's house. The skull had straight, parallel horns, about 20 inches (50 centimeters) long. It came from a "mountain goat," the hunter said, but the horns were unlike those of any goat MacKinnon had ever seen.

He asked in other villages about the animal, and was shown other skulls as well as dried skins of the animal. The Hmong people who hunted in the area called it *saht supahp*, which means "the polite animal," because it walks so quietly through the forest. From people living north of the Vu Quang Nature Reserve, MacKinnon learned that the animal was called *saola*, which means "spindle horn." Its horns look like wooden spindles used in weaving cloth.

The biologists learned that the saola lives on steep, heavily forested slopes. It is bigger than a goat but smaller than a cow, and has a dark brown coat and white markings on its face. They concluded that it was a new species—and a remarkable discovery. New kinds of rodents and

other small mammals are found every year, but an adult saola weighs over 200 pounds (90 kilograms). It was the biggest new species of mammal discovered in more than fifty years.

In 1994, Hmong hunters caught a few saolas, but they did not live long in captivity. An adult female saola died in a Laotian zoo just two weeks after her capture. Because there may be only two hundred saola in existence in Laos and Vietnam, the Vietnamese government has declared it an endangered species. The government also increased the size of the Vu Quang Nature Reserve. This helps protect not only the saola but also other wildlife of the reserve, including leopards, Malayan sun bears, tigers, sambar deer, and gaurs (wild oxen). And it gives some protection to yet another new species of mammal that was identified in the nature reserve—the large-antlered muntjac. It is a barking deer, a mammal with doglike fangs that weighs about 100 pounds (45 kilograms).

THE STRIPED RABBIT OF LAOS

The Vu Quang Nature Reserve, home of the large-antlered muntjac and the saola, lies in the Annamite Mountains. This rugged mountain chain forms a natural border between Vietnam and Laos. Until the 1990s, large areas of the Annamites were unexplored by biologists.

Several new species have been found. As is usually the case—for example, with the saola—the animal was unknown to scientists but familiar to local residents. When searching for new species, biologists

have found it useful to talk to hunters and to see what creatures are for sale in village food markets.

One day in 1998, biologist Robert Timmins of the Wildlife Conservation Society traveled to a village in Laos to buy supplies for his field work and to examine wildlife in its food market. There he saw a dead rabbit for sale. It had a dark brown stripe on the center of its forehead, and other bold, dark stripes on its body. Only one kind of rabbit with stripes was known in the world. It lives on the island of Sumatra, almost a thousand miles from Laos. That species and the newly discovered one could be considered distant cousins. Genetic evidence has confirmed that the two rabbit species are related. Biologists have seen the striped rabbit of Laos and Vietnam in the wild and are beginning to learn abut its life.

THE ACROBAT BIRD OF BRAZIL

Each year, biologists travel far from cities and good roads in order to search remote forests for bird species new to science. In 1994, however, an unusual bird was found living in cocoa plantations near densely populated areas in eastern Brazil. Some of its nests were built in trees within sight of a major highway, yet this bird was unknown to ornithologists.

The bird was first identified in 1994 by two Brazilian ornithologists, Paolo Sérgio Fonseca and Fernando Pacheco. They quickly told Bret Whitney, an ornithologist from Louisiana State University who had been searching out unknown birdlife in tropical forests. Whitney explained that the bird had been overlooked "because it stays way up in the canopy and its nest was confused with that of another species." The newly discovered bird is the pink-legged graveteiro. Its feathers are black and gray, and its bill and legs are pink. It is sometimes called "acrobata," because it often swings beneath leaves and the underside of branches as it hunts for insects and spiders. The name *graveteiro* means "twig gatherer" in Portuguese, the language of Brazil. Graveteiros gather hundreds of twigs and build large covered nests, placed near the tops of the tallest trees, sometimes as high as 140 feet (42 meters) above ground.

The pink-legged graveteiro lives in an area of eastern Brazil where most of the forests have been cut down. Tall trees remain over cocoa plantations, however, because cocoa grows well in partial shade. The tall trees shading the cocoa, the only remaining part of the native

forest, have allowed the pink-legged graveteiro and many other species of wildlife to survive.

Beginning in the late 1980s, a fungus called witch's broom began to spread through Brazil's cocoa plantations. This destructive pest has caused many landowners to stop growing cocoa. When they convert the land to other uses, the tall trees over cocoa plantations are usually cut down.

In eastern Brazil, conservation groups are trying to save some large blocks of forested land, including cocoa plantations. They hope to preserve enough habitat to ensure the survival of many creatures of the forest canopy, including the pink-legged graveteiro.

CAVE CREATURES OF ROMANIA

Since the early 1990s, biologists have been exploring a Romanian cave that was discovered in 1986 by workers building a power plant. Located near the Black Sea, Movile Cave is about 160 feet (48 m) deep and 800 feet (240 m) long. It is not full of spectacular stalactites that would make it a tourist attraction, but is, however, full of living treasures, including more than thirty new animal species.

Scientists estimate that the cave was cut off from the surface more than five million years ago. Life in the cave is nourished by hydrogen sulfide rising into water from great depth underground. Bacteria get chemical energy from the hydrogen sulfide, and the bacteria are the foundation of a food chain—animals that eat bacteria are eaten by other animals.

No fish or other animals with backbones have been found in Movile Cave. Every creature is an invertebrate—and every creature is blind. Some have very large antennae that enable them to find their way and find food. The animals include leeches, centipedes, spiders, earthworms, pill bugs, and water scorpions.

A team of Romanian and American scientists (from the University of Cincinnati) have studied the life of Movile Cave. By the end of the year 2000 they had identified forty-eight species, thirty-three of which had been unknown to science. Movile Cave is especially valuable to researchers because all of its life depends on hydrogen sulfide. The same is true of tube worms and other creatures that gather around vents on the ocean floor. Biologist Thomas Kane of the University of

Cincinnati said, "The great advantage of this cave over deep-ocean vents is that it is easily accessible. We can experiment in ways that would be prohibitively expensive in the deep sea."

THE DINGISO OF NEW GUINEA

Early in his childhood, Tim Flannery became intrigued with New Guinea, the large island north of his birthplace, Australia. At age 26 he went to New Guinea as a research scientist. He has returned again and again, exploring mountains and forests where no biologist had stepped before. He has identified more than 20 new species, including tree kangaroos, bats, bandicoots, and the world's largest rat. He wrote the very first book about the island's mammals.

In 1998 Flannery wrote, "I have always worried that my book *Mammals of New Guinea* would lead students into imagining that the age of exploration is finished in New Guinea. The book looks so glossy, so neat and so complete, but it is, in reality, just a beginning. New Guinea is as vast a field for adventure and discovery as it ever was."

One of Tim Flannery's most remarkable discoveries was the dingiso, a black-and-white tree kangaroo that lives in the Sudirman mountains of Irian Jaya, the Indonesian half of New Guinea. The first clue that such a mammal existed came to him in 1990, when a hunter gave him a jawbone unlike that of known tree kangaroos. Later that year he saw a Dani tribesman wearing a hat made of unusual fur, possibly from a tree kangaroo. He bought the hat. About a year later he was sent a photograph of a joey (young kangaroo) with strange black-and-white markings.

In May 1994, Flannery traveled to the Tembagapura area where the joey had been photographed. It is one of the least explored regions of Irian Jaya. There he showed the photo of the joey to a member of the

Moni tribe who lived in the area. The man immediately gave the Moni name for the black-and-white tree kangaroo: *dingiso.*

For the next several days Tim Flannery and hired hunters searched the forested mountains for a dingiso, without success. He decided to try higher in the mountains, where the trees were shorter. One hunter headed into even higher elevations. In a few days he returned with his hunting dogs, smiling and signaling that he had two tree kangaroos in a sack.

When Flannery saw the contents of the sack he felt "near-simulaneous sensations of exhilaration and despair." All it contained were pieces of skin and bones. Most of the kangaroos had been eaten by the hunter! Nevertheless, enough remained to establish the dingiso as a new species—one quite different from other tree kangaroos. It is the only black-and-white kangaroo, and its leg bones are not nearly as strong as those of other tree kangaroos. The dingiso cannot leap from treetops to the ground, as other tree kangaroos do. Although it is in the tree kangaroo family, it spends most of its time on the ground.

Eventually, Tim Flannery saw a whole dead dingiso, and live ones, too. The dingiso stands two and a half feet (about a meter) tall, and weighs about twenty pounds (9 kg). It is so tame that it sometimes approaches hunters when offered tasty leaves. The dingiso is rare in the mountain areas inhabited by the Dani tribe, which hunt it. However, it is common in the territory of the Moni people. Most Moni clans do not hunt the dingiso. It is thought to be an ancestor.

Speaking of the dingiso, a Moni elder said, "This animal is my nose"—meaning it was the center of his being. Tim Flannery hopes that such beliefs will help the dingiso survive.

THE LEAF DEER OF MYANMAR

West of Thailand lies Myanmar, the country formerly called Burma. These names—Burma or Myanmar—bring to mind pictures of tropical rain forests, but northern Myanmar borders Tibet and the Himalaya Mountains. In this remote region there are a great variety of habitats. The first zoological survey of the area was conducted in 1997 by a team of fifteen Burmese scientists and forestry officials. They were accompanied by Alan Rabinowitz, the Wildlife Conservation Society's director of science in Asia.

They hiked more than 200 miles (320 kilometers) through a spectacular landscape. "Between valleys and mountain passes," Rabinowitz recalls, "we followed trails that climbed precipitously from 1,500 to more than 10,000 feet." The expedition found red pandas and other species whose numbers have declined elsewhere. "We discovered species, such as blue sheep and stone marten, that had never been recorded as existing in Myanmar. One of the most exciting discoveries was the black barking deer, a species known at the time only from a mountainous pocket in southeastern China more than a thousand miles away."

In a small village Alan Rabinowitz also found the first clues to another, unknown species. On a hunter's "trophy board" hung several small skulls of a deer. The hunter said they were from a *hpet gyi*, or leaf deer, that lived on mountaintops.

Hiking on a trail several days later, Rabinowitz met a hunter carrying a small red deer he had shot with a crossbow. Because of its

small size, the biologist thought the deer was probably a juvenile common barking deer of the region. "I pried open the animal's mouth to examine its teeth, and froze. This little deer was no juvenile. It was an old adult!"

It was a leaf deer, said the hunter. Rabinowitz bought it from him— the first specimen to be collected and preserved for a science museum. Later genetic tests on cells from its body confirmed that it was unlike any other known barking deer. On a 1998 expedition, Alan Rabinowitz saw and examined a dozen other leaf deer killed by hunters.

The leaf deer, he learned, eats mostly fruit. It stands not quite two feet (60 cm) tall and weighs less than twenty-five pounds (11 kg). It is the second smallest deer in the world and lives only in dense forests of low mountain elevations in a small area of northern Myanmar. Study of the leaf deer's genetics reveals that it is the most primitive species of all living deer.

Local hunters were killing many leaf deer and other wildlife species. They traded skins, skulls, and other parts for such basic needs as clothing, tea, and salt. There are no natural sources of salt in northern Myanmar, and people mix salt with tea and also use it in cooking. In 1998, encouraged by Alan Rabinowitz, the Myanmar government established the huge Hkakabo Razi National Park in the area. The park staff provides local people with regular supplies of salt and other necessities. This program is aimed at curtailing the killing of the leaf deer and many other wild creatures of northern Myanmar.

MARMOSETS OF BRAZIL

In 1990, biologists Maria Lorini and Vanessa Persson of Brazil's Capao da Imbuia Natural History Museum set out to survey the birdlife of Superagui, a small island off the Brazilian coast. Local fishermen told them of a monkey that lived in the island's forests. The biologists investigated and discovered an unknown species: the caissara, or black-faced lion tamarin monkey.

Since its discovery, a population of this species has also been found living on the Brazilian mainland. Like the golden lion tamarin and the woolly spider monkey, this species is threatened with extinction. Brazil's Atlantic coastal forest once covered 400,000 square miles (1,040,000 square kilometers). Now about two percent remains. The fate of the remaining forest will determine that of the monkeys and other species that rely on this unique habitat.

As it turned out, the discovery of the caissara monkey was just the first of a remarkable decade. By the year 2000, ten more monkey species had been identified in Brazil. This brought the total of known primate species in Brazil to seventy-nine. (Primates include humans, gorillas, chimpanzees, and monkeys.) With a quarter of all known species, Brazil is home to the greatest diversity of primates on Earth.

The new primate species, all squirrel-size marmosets, were discovered by biologists working for Conservation International. It is a leading group in the search for areas of rich biodiversity. In 1996, Russell Mittermeier, president of Conservation International, announced the discovery of the Satere marmoset. It was found in

forests of the central Amazon region, between the Madeira and Tapajos Rivers, and was named for the Satere people who live there.

"Finding a new beetle in the rain forest may not be surprising, but finding a new monkey is truly exciting," said Russell Mittermeier. "It also shows how ignorant we are of the vast range of life on Earth." He added, "I wouldn't be surprised if we found another five monkeys by the year 2000."

That is exactly what happened. In 1997 one the tiniest monkeys on Earth was identified in Brazil. This little marmoset is just four inches (10 cm) long and weighs 6.5 ounces (190 g). It was found by primatologist Marc van Roosmalen of the National Institute for Amazon Research in Manaus, Brazil.

Marc van Roosmalen often explores remote areas of the Amazon for Conservation International. In early 2000, that organization announced the discovery of more new species of marmoset. Marc van Roosmalen had noticed unusual monkeys being kept as pets in small riverbank settlements in northwestern Brazil. There were two kinds, both with almost white fur. One had orange-yellow underparts and a cap of light gray fur on its head; the other had a gray back and a bright orange patch at the tip of its black tail. Both were new marmoset species.

Russell Mittermeier said, "These findings remind us of how much [we] have yet to learn about the earth's diversity of life. Even among our closest relatives, the primates, there are still new species to be discovered."

UNDISCOVERED TREASURES

With so many discoveries of animals new to science, some people may hope that the Loch Ness monster and Big Foot will soon be captured. However, the areas where people report seeing these "creatures" have been thoroughly searched. Photographs and films offered as vital evidence of their existence have been proved to be hoaxes. No doubt some people will continue to wish that Big Foot and other mythical creatures exist. In the meantime biologists continue to discover fascinating *real* animals.

The main search sites continue to be remote regions of tropical forests. Biologists often travel by boat or overland in roadless areas for several days in order to reach places where few or no scientists have ever set foot. Their reward: the very next orchid, beetle, or lizard they see might be an unknown species.

These expeditions can be a physical ordeal, but attempts to explore other habitats for unknown life are challenging in other ways. In the Arctic, for example, scientists are drilling into ancient permafrost (earth that is frozen year round) and finding unusual living bacteria, fungi, algae, and other microscopic organisms. At the opposite end of the planet, researchers are carefully planning exploration of a lake that lies beneath 2.5 miles (4 kilometers) of ice in Antarctica. The water of Lake Vostok—about the size of Lake Ontario (one of the Great Lakes that lie between the United States and Canada)—has been sealed off from the rest of the world for millions of years. Biologists have reason to believe that bacteria and other microbes live in Lake

Vostok. Space scientists are especially curious about this exploration, because humans may someday search for signs of life in an ice-covered ocean thought to exist on Europa, one of Jupiter's moons.

Scientists from several nations have cooperated in an ice-drilling project that stopped within 400 feet (120 meters) of Lake Vostok. The final drilling that actually reaches the lake will be done with great care and special equipment so that samples of the water and its life will not be contaminated with microbes from the Antarctic surface.

The waters surrounding the Antarctic continent are also being explored as never before. Surprising numbers of new fish species have been discovered. Like many fish near Antarctica, they have antifreeze proteins in their blood that keep them from turning into blocks of ice.

Elsewhere on Earth, the ocean depths remain as the last great unexplored wilderness. Cold and dark, these waters were once considered to be almost lifeless. Now scientists believe they are home to an astonishing variety of life—perhaps ten times the number of species found on land.

The development of small research submarines has enabled scientists to explore and collect samples far beneath the surface. Using the submersible Alvin in 1977, scientists at a depth of 1.5 miles (2.4 km) discovered vents spewing hot, mineral-laden water from the ocean floor. Since then, these hydrothermal vents have been found all over the world. They teem with life, including blind crabs and shrimp, giant white clams, zoarcid fish, and tube worms. Many are new species. Researchers have discovered that 10-foot- (3-m)-long tube worms living on the floor of the Gulf of Mexico are up to 250 years old, a record for creatures without backbones.

Hydrothermal vents are like oases on the sea floor, but scientists using new methods of collecting samples from the deep have also found thousands of new species on the open sea bottom. In the mid-1980s scientists began lowering devices called box corers to the ocean floor. These boxes cut into a 1-foot (30-cm) square of the bottom, then close up so nothing is lost when the box is pulled up to the surface. Since the box corer itself is small, it catches mostly small creatures. Some are fish, but most are invertebrates. They include new species of sea worms, brachiopods, sea cucumbers, crustaceans, and brittle sea stars. New species were found in nearly every sample taken from the ocean bottom. It takes biologists years to identify all of the life collected—and only a tiny fraction of the ocean depths have been sampled. A great treasure of biodiversity remains to be discovered.

People will always be curious about the other living things that share Earth. For scientists, just discovering new organisms and figuring out how they live is reward enough. There are, however, practical reasons for discovering—and protecting—Earth's biodiversity. Both plants and animals have chemicals within their bodies that defend them against disease and enemies. These same chemicals may someday be vital in the development of drugs that protect humans from germs and viruses, or from the growth of cancers.

Whether for selfish reasons or for simple human curiosity, the quest for species new to science continues, full of challenge and adventure.

PROTECTING EARTH'S BIODIVERSITY

Discovering a new species, or finding one that was thought to be extinct, is a remarkable event that is all too often followed by the challenge of saving the species from dying out. Part of the challenge is not just establishing a national park or nature reserve to protect the species' habitat, but ensuring that local people benefit from it.

A successful example is a park established in Madagascar, the large island east of Africa that is rich in unique plants and animals. More than eighty percent of this nation's forests have been cut down, and half of Madagascar's thirty-two species of lemurs have already become extinct. A lemur researcher, Patricia Wright, worked for several years to convince others and raise money for the establishment of Ranomafana National Park. To help ensure the park's protection, local villagers receive half of its entrance fees paid by tourists and hold more than a hundred park jobs. They also benefit from new schools and health clinics that were built in their communities near the park.

In ways like this, conservation groups are working to halt the loss of Earth's precious diversity of life by protecting the wild habitats that remain. The groups include:

African Wildlife Foundation
1400 16th St.,NW
Washington, D.C.
www.awf.org

Conservation International
1919 M St., NW
Washington, D.C. 20036
www.conservation.org

Institute for the Conservation of Tropical Environments
State University of New York at Stony Brook
Stony Brook, NY 11794

Nature Conservancy
1815 North Lynn St.
Arlington, VA 22209
www.nature.org

Primate Conservation, Inc.,
1411 Shannock Road, Charlestown
RI 02813-3627
www.primate.org

Rainforest Action Network
450 Sansome, Suite 700
San Francisco, CA 94111
www.ran.org/ran/

Rainforest Alliance
65 Bleecker Street
New York, NY 10012

Wildlife Conservation Society
185th St. & Southern Blvd.

Bronx, NY 10460-1099
www.wcs.org

World Wildlife Fund
1250 24th St. NW
Washington, D.C.
www.worldwildlife.org